FROM WOUNDED TO WONDERFUL

A COMPREHENSIVE GUIDE TO HEALING FROM HEARTBREAK

Copyright © 2023, Sunshine Within, LLC
All rights reserved. No portion of this book may be reproduced in any form without permission from the publisher, except as permitted by U.S. copyright law. For permissions, contact: urlight@sunshinewithin.org

FROM WOUNDED TO WONDERFUL

A COMPREHENSIVE GUIDE TO HEALING FROM HEARTBREAK

Even a flower must have its shell broken from the seed in order to grow. Without that "brokeness", we would not be able to experience the beauty that was held within that seed. Even after that seedling has escaped from the shell, it still must find its way through the darkness and break through the surface of the soil. Growing in the darkness and emerging as new.

YOU are growing despite your pain. YOU are learning your way through the darkness. YOU are healing so you can emerge as new. YOU are a flower.

Do not ever forget that.

Contents

Introduction..

Ch. 1: Understanding Emotional Heartbreak..

Ch. 2: The Journey Within: Self-Reflection..

Ch. 3: Breaking Free from People-Pleasing..

Ch. 4: Redefining Success in Relationships..

Ch. 5: Cultivating Self-Esteem and Self-Love..

Ch. 6: Healthy Relationship Mindset..

Ch. 7: Tools for Emotional Healing..

Ch. 8: Realizing Your Wonderful Self..

Ch. 9: This Is NOT the End..

Introduction

There are a unique set of emotional challenges that single women find themselves navigating during their mid-40s to mid-50s. As they reach this stage of life, societal expectations and personal aspirations may collide, leading to introspection and a heightened awareness of unfulfilled romantic desires. These women often carry the weight of past disappointments, unmet expectations, and societal pressures, which can intensify emotional heartbreak. The complexities of singlehood in this age group involve reconciling personal accomplishments with the perceived societal benchmarks, often leaving them questioning their self-worth and struggling with feelings of isolation.

The emotional well-being of an individual is a crucial aspect of overall health and happiness. Emotional heartbreak can have a profound impact on various aspects of life, affecting self-esteem, relationships, and overall life satisfaction. Unresolved emotional issues can lead to a cycle of negative thinking, self-doubt, and hindered personal growth. By addressing emotional heartbreak and regaining control of emotional health, these individuals can pave the way for a more fulfilling and rewarding future. This not only impacts their personal happiness but also influences the quality of their relationships and interactions with the world.

Does any of this sound familiar to you? If so, this guide is for you.

By exploring these challenges, you will embark on a transformative journey towards emotional healing and self-empowerment by providing insights and practical strategies for overcoming various stages of emotional heartbreak. The ultimate goal is to shift your perspective from one marked by wounds and insecurities to a more positive, resilient, and wonderful outlook. Through self-reflection, empowerment, and cultivating a healthy mindset, you will be equipped to embrace your own worth and create a healthy foundation for fulfilling relationships, not just romantic. This guide serves as a roadmap for reclaiming control of your emotional health and fostering a positive transformation toward a more wonderful self.

Chapter 1:
Understanding Emotional Heartbreak

Understanding Emotional Heartbreak

Exploring the unique challenges of the constantly broken hearted

Single women in their mid-40s to mid-50s face a distinctive set of challenges that come from the overlap of personal and societal expectations. During this timeframe, many individuals may reflect on their life choices, and for single women, this can lead to a heightened awareness of unmet romantic dreams. The pressure to conform to societal norms, coupled with the expectations of family and friends, can create a sense of isolation and inadequacy. Exploring these challenges involves acknowledging the complexity of balancing personal achievements with societal expectations, and addressing the emotional toll that this internal conflict can take on their well-being.

The impact of past experiences on current emotional well-being

Emotional heartbreak often stems from past experiences, including failed relationships, unfulfilled expectations, and the societal stigma often attached to singlehood. These experiences can create emotional wounds that linger, influencing current emotional well-being. Understanding the impact of these past experiences is crucial for healing. It is important to acknowledge and understand the ways in which past relationships and societal, and possibly cultural expectations may have contributed to emotional baggage, affecting self-esteem, trust, and the ability to form new connections. Recognizing the connection between past experiences and present emotions is a key step toward initiating the healing process.

Common self-esteem issues and people-pleasing tendencies

Many single women in this demographic struggle with self-esteem issues rooted in socictal expectations and personal comparisons. The absence of a long-term romantic relationship can sometimes be misconstrued as a personal failure, leading to feelings of inadequacy and self-doubt. Additionally, the desire for acceptance and fear of judgment can manifest in people-pleasing tendencies. It is critical to address common self-esteem issues, such as negative self-talk and the internalization of societal norms. All of which leads to the detrimental impact of lacking personal boundaries and the inability to prioritize self-care. Recognizing and addressing these tendencies are essential steps toward regaining control of emotional health and fostering a more positive self-image.

Chapter 2:

The Journey Within: Self-Reflection

The Journey Within: Self-Reflection

Encouraging self-awareness and honest introspection:
Self-awareness is the first step in the journey toward emotional healing. This involves fostering a genuine understanding of your thoughts, emotions, and behaviors. Being able to engage in honest introspection and true exploration of beliefs regarding relationships, self-worth, and societal expectations are all parts of the foundation of self-awareness. It is necessary to identify areas that require attention and gain clarity on their values and desires within your life. This can be accomplished in a variety of ways.

1. Mindful Breathing for Emotional Release:
   - Find a quiet space to sit comfortably.
   - Close your eyes and take slow, deep breaths.
   - As you exhale, visualize releasing the emotional pain with each breath.
   - Focus on the sensation of breath entering and leaving your body.
   - Allow yourself to feel and acknowledge the emotions without judgment.

2. Journaling for Emotional Processing:
   - Set aside dedicated time for journaling each day.
   - Write about your feelings, thoughts, and experiences related to the heartbreak.
   - Express yourself freely without concern for grammar or structure.
   - Reflect on patterns or triggers that emerge from your writing.
   - Use the journal as a safe space to explore and release pent-up emotions.

3. Loving-Kindness Meditation:
   - Sit comfortably and close your eyes.
   - Begin by extending feelings of love and compassion toward yourself.
   - Gradually extend these feelings to others, including those involved in the heartbreak.
   - Envision healing and well-being for yourself and all parties.
   - This practice fosters self-compassion and a sense of interconnectedness.

4. Body Scan for Emotional Awareness:
   - Lie down and bring attention to different parts of your body.

- Notice physical sensations without judgment.
- Identify areas of tension or discomfort related to emotional distress.
- Breathe into those areas, allowing them to soften and release.
- This practice helps connect emotional experiences with bodily sensations.

5. Gratitude Practice for Positive Shifts:
- Each day, identify three things you are grateful for.
- Focus on aspects of your life unrelated to the heartbreak.
- This practice helps shift the focus toward positive aspects, fostering a more balanced perspective.

Approach these exercises with gentleness and patience, allowing the healing process to unfold gradually. Consistent practice can lead to increased self-awareness and a deeper connection with one's inner self. It will be important for you to practice all of these techniques to become more familiar with them. Although some of these strategies may not be new to you, embrace them with open arms and new eyes. You may surprise yourself. This is the beginning of your chance to revisit previous techniques that may not have served you at the time but will now unlock a portion of you that you may have overlooked before.

Identifying patterns of behavior and thinking that contribute to emotional heartbreak:

Building on self-awareness, it is important to identify patterns that contribute to emotional heartbreak. Are you able to recognize recurring behaviors, thoughts, and beliefs that may be hindering your emotional well-being? This involves examining past relationships, exploring how societal expectations have influenced decision-making, and uncovering any self-sabotaging behaviors. By pinpointing these patterns, you can begin to break the cycle of emotional heartbreak and make conscious choices aligned with your authentic self. Do not think this is a time to beat yourself up for not recognizing patterns sooner. This is you taking the time, an honest introspection, to see how you operate in romantic situations. More often than not, the decisions you made made sense at the time. There were a variety of choices, decisions, and factors that all played into whatever it is that happened. At that time, you made the best decision and choice for yourself. Now, being able to look back at it all, what do you see now? What were you overlooking? Not just from your partner but from yourself as well. It is necessary to address where certain behaviors from yourself stemmed. Ask yourself is the behavior new or has it appeared previously? If it has appeared previously, what was that relationship like? How did it make you feel? Have you felt those feelings before? If so, who made you feel that way? What was that situation? Asking yourself those hard questions to get to the root of your emotional framework takes time. It is not easy. It can uncover a lot but also help you to see a lot as well. It is possible to realize some of your emotional heartbreak may not have begun from a romantic relationship.

Journaling exercises for self-reflection and personal growth:

To facilitate the self-reflection process, journaling exercises is a powerful tool for personal growth. With prompts and structured activities designed to guide you through the exploration of your thoughts and emotions, journaling can serve as a cathartic outlet for expressing feelings, recording insights gained through self-reflection, and tracking progress on the journey toward healing. The goal is to allow you to see your strength documented through your experiences, track your emotional evolution, and gain a deeper understanding of yourself as you work towards shifting your perspective from wounded to wonderful.

Here are some journal prompts and structured activities designed to guide you through this process. If journaling is already an activity you do, challenge yourself to answer these questions. These prompts may lead you to discover or uncover emotions, thought processes, or actions that you previously overlooked from yourself or about yourself. They may lead you to ask even deeper questions to yourself.

1. Reflection on the Relationship:
   - What were the positive aspects of the relationship?
   - What were the challenges or red flags you may have overlooked?
   - How did you contribute to the dynamics of the relationship?

2. Identifying Personal Strengths:
   - List three qualities about yourself that you value.
   - Reflect on moments when you demonstrated resilience.
   - Identify strengths that can contribute to your healing and growth.

3. Forgiveness and Letting Go:
   - Write a letter to yourself forgiving any perceived mistakes.
   - Write a letter to the person involved expressing forgiveness (you don't have to send it).
   - Reflect on how forgiveness can contribute to your healing.

4. Vision for the Future:
   - Envision your ideal self post-healing. What does she look like emotionally, mentally, and physically?
   - Describe the kind of relationship you aspire to have in the future.
   - Outline steps to work towards this vision.

5. Self-Care Planning:
   - Create a self-care plan for the week, including activities that bring you joy.
   - Reflect on how each activity contributes to your well-being.
   - Adjust the plan based on what works best for you.

6. Boundaries Exploration:
   - Identify areas where you need to establish or reinforce boundaries.
   - Reflect on how setting and maintaining boundaries can contribute to your emotional well-being.
   - List specific actions you can take to communicate and enforce these boundaries.

Approach journaling with an open heart and a sense of curiosity. Your progress is a gradual process. Each entry contributes to your journey of healing and personal growth. Taking the time to be open and honest with yourself is imperative to true and sustained personal growth. Your journal is a no judgment zone. Embrace all of who you are within the pages of your journal. Give a voice to those stifled emotions. Allow them to be free.

There is nothing wrong…nothing bad…nothing too much…nothing not enough. You are everything you need to be. YOU are enough. All of the journaling will allow you to see in writing just how amazing you truly are.

Chapter 3:

Breaking Free from People-Pleasing

Breaking Free from People-Pleasing

Recognizing the negative impact of people-pleasing on emotional health:
More often than not, you likely want others around you to be happy. You may have gotten to the point that your own identity has become wrapped up in the notion that you are easygoing and agreeable. Maybe not always but the majority of the time you may be viewed in this manner by others. You may even thrive on bringing joy to others. Bringing joy to others is not a bad thing. It is a beautiful thing. However, the frequent need for external validation and the fear of disappointing others can lead to a depletion of one's own emotional resources. Sometimes resulting in feelings of guilt if you choose yourself over someone else's wants. By recognizing the negative impact of people-pleasing on self-esteem and overall emotional health, you will be able to confront these patterns and understand the importance of prioritizing your own needs. Pay attention to the patterns that are the most familiar to you. Here's how this dynamic unfolds:

1. Dependency on External Approval:
 - When someone often seeks validation from others, their sense of self-worth becomes heavily reliant on external feedback.
 - Approval, praise, or positive feedback from others become essential for validating their identity and self-esteem.
 - This dependency creates vulnerability because the individual's emotional state is contingent on the opinions and judgments of others.

2. Fear of Disappointing Others:
 - The fear of disappointing others can be rooted in the desire to maintain positive external validation.
 - This fear may lead individuals to prioritize others' expectations over their own needs, wants, or authentic expression.
 - The constant pressure to meet perceived expectations can generate anxiety and stress, further impacting emotional well-being.

3. Exhaustion from Overcommitment:
- Individuals driven by a fear of disappointment may find themselves overcommitting to meet others' expectations.
- This overextension of time, energy, and resources can lead to exhaustion and burnout as they strive to fulfill external demands at the expense of their own well-being.

4. Neglecting Personal Needs:
- The pursuit of external validation may result in neglecting one's own needs, desires, and boundaries.
- Individuals may compromise their values or engage in behaviors that align with external expectations but conflict with their authentic selves.
- Neglecting personal needs and authenticity can lead to a gradual erosion of inner satisfaction and fulfillment.

5. Erosion of Authenticity:
- The constant quest for external validation can contribute to a loss of authenticity.
- Individuals may adapt their behaviors, opinions, or choices to align with what they believe will please others rather than expressing their true selves.
- This erosion of authenticity can lead to feelings of disconnection from one's true identity, contributing to emotional distress.

6. Impact on Emotional Resilience:
- Over time, the depletion of emotional resources resulting from seeking external validation and fearing disappointment can weaken emotional resilience.
- Individuals may struggle to cope with setbacks or criticism, as their emotional well-being is closely tied to external factors.
- A lack of internal validation and self-compassion can make it challenging to navigate life's challenges effectively.

To address these challenges, you may benefit from establishing a more internalized sense of validation, developing self-compassion, and learning to set healthy boundaries. Building emotional resilience involves creating a deep connection with your authentic self, independent of external judgments or expectations. Recognizing the importance of self-care and prioritizing your well-being is crucial for maintaining emotional balance and a sense of fulfillment. Journaling how these patterns have exhibited themselves within your life will help you reveal some underlying habits and patterns within your relationships.

Setting healthy boundaries in personal and professional relationships:

In order to effectively break free from people-pleasing involves the establishment of healthy boundaries. This section provides practical guidance on identifying and communicating personal limits in both personal and professional relationships. Strategies for effectively communicating boundaries are explored, helping you navigate potentially challenging conversations with confidence.

Identifying Personal Limits:
1. Self-Reflection:
   - Take time to reflect on your own needs, values, and priorities.
   - Identify situations or behaviors that make you uncomfortable or trigger negative emotions.
   - Consider past experiences where you felt your boundaries were violated.

2. Pay Attention to Emotions:
   - Tune into your emotional responses in different situations.
   - Feelings of discomfort, resentment, or stress may indicate a need for stronger boundaries.
   - Positive emotions in certain contexts can highlight areas where your boundaries are respected and valued.

3. Physical and Emotional Cues:
   - Notice physical sensations and emotions when interacting with others.
   - Feelings of tension, unease, or fatigue may be signs that your boundaries are being challenged.
   - Listen to your intuition and trust your instincts about what feels right or wrong.

Communicating Boundaries:
1. Be Clear and Specific:
 - Clearly articulate your boundaries using specific language.
 - Instead of vague statements, provide concrete examples of behaviors that are acceptable or not acceptable.
 - For example, say, "I need uninterrupted time in the evenings for self-care, so please avoid calling after 8 PM."

2. Use "I" Statements:
 - Frame your boundaries using "I" statements to express your needs without sounding accusatory.
 - For instance, say, "I need some quiet time to recharge after work," instead of, "You always interrupt my alone time."

3. Express Consequences:
 - Clearly communicate the consequences of crossing boundaries.
 - This helps others understand the importance of your limits.
 - For instance, "If I feel overwhelmed, I may need to take a break from socializing to recharge."

4. Choose Appropriate Timing:
 - Select an appropriate time to discuss boundaries when you and the other person are calm and focused.
 - Avoid addressing boundaries in the heat of an argument.
 - Schedule a separate conversation to ensure it receives the attention it deserves.

Strategies for Boundary Maintenance:
1. Consistency is Key:
 - Consistently enforce your boundaries to establish a pattern of behavior.
 - Be firm in maintaining your limits even if it feels uncomfortable initially.
 - Consistency helps others understand the importance of respecting your boundaries.

2. Regularly Reassess:
 - Periodically reassess your boundaries to ensure they align with your current needs and circumstances.

- Life changes, and so can your requirements for personal space and emotional well-being.

3. Seek Support:
   - Share your boundary-setting journey with trusted friends or a mentor.
   - Seek advice on how to effectively communicate and reinforce your boundaries.
   - Having a support system can provide encouragement and guidance.

4. Practice Self-Compassion:
   - Understand that setting boundaries is an ongoing process.
   - Be kind to yourself if you face challenges or encounter resistance from others.
   - Acknowledge your progress and celebrate small victories in maintaining healthy boundaries.

Recognizing the importance of boundaries, learning effective communication strategies, and emphasizing the ongoing nature of boundary-setting will contribute to healthier and more respectful relationships. Do not overlook the relationship you are building with and within yourself as well. You will need to recognize, learn, and respect your own personal boundaries.

Learning to say "no" without guilt and embracing self-care practices:
   Central to breaking free from people-pleasing is the ability to assertively say "no" without succumbing to guilt. This section addresses the internal barriers that may make it challenging for you to decline requests or invitations. Practical techniques, such as assertiveness training and communication tips, are provided to help you set boundaries gracefully and respectfully. You will be guided to explore and incorporate self-care activities that align with your personal preferences, promoting resilience and well-being. Allowing you to embrace self-care practices as an essential component of reclaiming your emotional health. Self-care is more than a spa day or some time with your friends. It is more than spending time alone with yourself doing a favorite activity. It is truly learning how to pour back into yourself. How to refill your empty cup unapologetically. Because some of these methods may be foreign to you or uncomfortable, it will be important to figure out how to practice these techniques and tips. You may have been the cheerleader for many others, now it is time to be your own cheerleader. You have the voice and you are worth all of the effort.

Internal Barriers to Saying "No":
1. Fear of Rejection:
   - *Barrier:* A deep-seated fear that saying "no" will lead to rejection or disapproval from others.
   - *Technique:* Remind yourself that your worth is not determined by others' approval. Practice self-validation and self-compassion.

2. Desire for Approval:
   - *Barrier:* The need for external validation and a fear of disappointing others.
   - *Technique:* Acknowledge that seeking constant approval can be draining. Focus on self-approval and recognize that setting boundaries is a form of self-respect.

3. Overcommitment Habit:
   - *Barrier:* A habitual pattern of overcommitting due to a desire to please others.
   - *Technique:* Gradually replace the habit of saying "yes" automatically with a pause. Take a moment to evaluate if the request aligns with your priorities and capacity.

4. Avoidance of Conflict:
   - *Barrier:* A reluctance to engage in conflict or discomfort that saying "no" might create.
   - *Technique:* Develop assertiveness skills to express your boundaries diplomatically. Practice assertive communication in low-stakes situations to build confidence.

Exploring and Incorporating Self-Care:
1. Identify Personal Preferences:
   - Reflect on activities that bring joy, relaxation, or fulfillment.
   - Consider hobbies, activities, or rituals that align with your values and preferences.

2. Create a Self-Care Plan:
   - Develop a personalized self-care plan with specific activities.
   - Schedule regular self-care time in your calendar to prioritize these activities.

3. Prioritize Well-Being:

- Recognize that self-care is not selfish; it's essential for well-being.
- Prioritize self-care activities as non-negotiable aspects of your routine.

4. Experiment and Adjust:
   - Try different self-care activities to discover what resonates with you.
   - Be open to adjusting your self-care routine based on changing needs and preferences.

5. Incorporate Daily Rituals:
   - Integrate small, daily rituals that promote relaxation and joy.
   - Whether it's a few minutes of mindful breathing or a morning routine, these rituals contribute to overall well-being.

Overcoming internal barriers, assertively communicating boundaries, and embracing self-care as a non-negotiable part of your life can create a firm foundation for resilience, well-being, and a healthier approach to relationships. Some of these techniques, strategies, and tips may be familiar or completely foreign but approaching them with open arms can give you the opportunity to learn something new about yourself. You truly are creating a voice for the portion of you that has been silenced for so long. This is not an easy process but you are here because you know how important you are. You know how much you deserve to be loved and heard and respected and seen.

Chapter 4:

Redefining Success in Relationships

Redefining Success in Relationships

Evaluating personal definitions of success in romantic relationships:
It is imperative to critically examine your pre-existing definitions of success in romantic relationships. This will prompt you to reflect on whether these definitions are based on societal norms, external pressures, or personal values. The goal is for you to establish authentic and personalized benchmarks for success in your romantic life.

Self-Discovery Activities for Clarifying Relationship Goals:
1. Create a Vision Board for an Ideal Relationship:
   - Gather magazines, images, and quotes that resonate with your vision of an ideal relationship.
   - Arrange them on a board, representing aspects like communication, shared interests, and emotional connection.
   - Reflect on the visual representation regularly to reinforce your relationship goals.

2. List Essential Qualities in a Partner:
   - Make a comprehensive list of qualities you value in a partner.
   - Categorize them into non-negotiables, preferences, and desirable qualities.
   - Use this list as a reference point when evaluating potential relationships.

3. Reflect on Past Relationships:
   - Journal about past relationships, noting patterns, successes, and areas for growth.
   - Identify qualities that contributed positively or negatively to your well-being.
   - Use this reflection to refine your understanding of what you want in future relationships.

4. Explore Your Values and Priorities:
   - Create a list of your core values and priorities in life.
   - Consider how these values align with your relationship goals.
   - Ensure that your vision of an ideal relationship aligns with your broader life values.

5. Consider Emotional Aspects:

- Reflect on the emotional aspects that contribute to a fulfilling connection.
   - Identify emotions such as trust, respect, affection, and shared joy that are crucial for you.
   - Consider how these emotions manifest in day-to-day interactions within a relationship.

6. Visualize Everyday Moments:
   - Close your eyes and visualize everyday moments in your ideal relationship.
   - Picture shared activities, communication styles, and emotional exchanges.
   - This visualization exercise can help clarify your desires and expectations.

7. Create a Relationship Manifesto:
   - Synthesize your reflections into a relationship manifesto or statement of intent.
   - Outline your values, goals, and desired dynamics in a future relationship.
   - Use this manifesto as a guide and reminder of your personalized benchmarks for success.

Approach these activities with openness and curiosity, viewing them as dynamic tools for self-discovery and empowerment in establishing authentic relationship goals.

Shifting focus from external validation to internal fulfillment:
   Shifting the focus from external validation to internal fulfillment is a pivotal step in the journey toward a healthier perspective on relationships. This section explores the dangers of seeking validation and happiness solely from external sources and the importance of cultivating internal sources of joy and contentment. Practical exercises, such as mindfulness practices and gratitude journaling are key in helping you redirect your focus inward. By encouraging the development of a strong sense of self-worth and fulfillment, you can begin to break free from the pressure to achieve traditional relationship milestones. Instead, you will learn how to create connections that align with your authentic self and forge the path that was meant for you.

Dangers of Seeking Validation and Happiness Exclusively from External Sources:

1. Vulnerability to External Judgments:
   - *Example:* Relying solely on external validation makes you susceptible to the opinions and judgments of others. If external approval diminishes, it can lead to feelings of inadequacy or unworthiness.

2. Conditional Happiness:
   - *Example:* Tying happiness exclusively to external circumstances, such as relationship status or societal expectations, results in a conditional form of joy. Any deviation from societal norms may disrupt this happiness.

3. Inconsistent Self-Worth:
   - *Example:* Depending on external validation for self-worth creates an inconsistent sense of value. When praised, self-worth may soar, but criticism or rejection can lead to a significant decline.

4. Strain on Relationships:
   - *Example:* Seeking validation solely from a romantic partner may strain the relationship. The constant need for approval can create unrealistic expectations, leading to misunderstandings and conflicts.

5. Loss of Authenticity:
   - *Example:* External validation may tempt you to conform to societal norms or expectations, resulting in the loss of authenticity. This conformity can lead to dissatisfaction and a sense of living a life that doesn't align with your personal values. Can you think of a recent example of this?

6. Neglect of Personal Growth:
   - *Example:* The pursuit of external validation might overshadow personal growth and development. You may prioritize conforming to expectations over pursuing goals that genuinely resonate with your authentic self.

Importance of Cultivating Internal Sources of Joy and Contentment:

1. Stable Self-Worth:
   - *Example:* Cultivating internal sources of joy fosters a stable and resilient sense of self-worth. Even in the absence of external validation, you can maintain a positive self-image based on your intrinsic value.

2. Authentic Happiness:
   - *Example:* Internal sources of joy derive from alignment with personal values and authentic experiences. This form of happiness is lasting and not contingent on external circumstances or societal benchmarks.

3. Empowerment and Autonomy:
   - *Example:* When joy comes from within, you feel empowered and in control of your emotional well-being. This autonomy allows for a more fulfilling and self-directed life.

4. Resilience in the Face of Challenges:
   - *Example:* Cultivating internal sources of contentment builds resilience. When faced with challenges, you can draw on internal strengths and coping mechanisms rather than relying solely on external support.

5. Enhanced Relationships:
   - *Example:* Building internal sources of joy positively impacts relationships. *__You__* bring a sense of fulfillment into your connections, reducing dependency on external validation from others.

6. Alignment with Personal Values:
- *Example:* Internal joy often stems from living in accordance with your values and priorities. This alignment fosters a sense of purpose and fulfillment that transcends societal expectations.

7. Embracing Life's Uniqueness:
- *Example:* By cultivating internal joy, you embrace the uniqueness of your life journey. You are less compelled to conform to traditional relationship milestones that may not align with who you truly are.

Breaking free from the reliance on external validation and societal expectations returns your power to you. This freedom allows you to create and nurture connections that genuinely align with your values and aspirations. Your focus shifts toward building internal joy and contentment, fostering a resilient and authentic approach to relationships and life.

Celebrating past successes in other areas of life and applying those lessons to relationships:

Building on the notion that success in relationships can be informed by success in other areas of life, you need to celebrate your achievements and victories in various domains. By recognizing and appreciating your accomplishments in your career, personal growth, and other aspects, you can draw valuable lessons and insights that can be applied to your romantic life. Although it may seem odd, being able to identify transferable skills and strengths and leveraging those qualities to navigate and enhance your relationships may be one of the puzzle pieces you have been missing. It's time to explore that further.

Chapter 5:

Cultivating Self-Esteem and Self-Love

Cultivating Self-Esteem and Self-Love

Building a positive self-image and embracing self-worth:

This section is dedicated to helping you through the process of building a positive self-image and embracing your inherent self-worth. Practical exercises, such as positive affirmations and self-appreciation journaling will help you recognize and celebrate your strengths and unique qualities. This will also help you understand the importance of reframing negative self-talk and challenging limiting beliefs that may have contributed to low self-esteem. By promoting a positive self-image, you lay the foundation for increased confidence and a more resilient sense of self. You are actively taking back control of your self and redefining who you are. Some of these exercises may be difficult in the beginning. Not because the exercise itself is difficult but because it will force you to look at your self, your inner self, in ways you have not done previously or at a depth never once before gone.

Exercises for Building a Positive Self-Image and Embracing Self-Worth:

1. Positive Affirmations:

- *Exercise:* Begin and end each day with positive affirmations. Stand in front of a mirror, look yourself in the eyes, and affirm your strengths, uniqueness, and worth. It may feel uncomfortable in the beginning but you are speaking to the part of you that is ignored and overlooked. You are speaking to the part of you that needs to be seen and loved. Speak to that part of you that has been hurt. Speak without question. Replace that negative voice in your head with the positive sound of your voice. Speak with gentleness and care. Speak with gentleness and care. Speak with assuredness.

  - *Example Affirmations:*
    - *"I am worthy of love and respect."*
    - *"I embrace my strengths and celebrate my uniqueness."*
    - *"I am confident and capable of overcoming challenges."*

2. Self-Appreciation Journaling:

- *Exercise:* Dedicate time each day to journal about your achievements, qualities, and moments of self-appreciation. Reflect on your resilience, accomplishments, and the positive impact you've had on others. This may feel time consuming at first but you are worth the time to explore and celebrate every part of who you are every day.

  - *Prompts:*

- *Write about a recent achievement and how it made you feel.*
  - *List three qualities about yourself that you appreciate.*
  - *Reflect on a challenge you overcame and the strengths you utilized.*

3. Strengths Assessment:
  - ***Exercise:*** Identify your core strengths and skills. Make a list of qualities that others appreciate about you and instances where you've excelled. Think about as many as you can. You likely have more strengths than you give yourself credit for.
  - ***Reflection Questions:***
    - *What are three strengths that others say I consistently demonstrate?*
    - *How have these strengths contributed to my personal and professional life?*
    - *In what ways can I further develop and utilize these strengths?*

4. Reframing Negative Self-Talk:
  - ***Exercise:*** Pay attention to negative self-talk and challenge those thoughts. When you catch yourself thinking negatively, reframe it into a positive or neutral statement.
  - ***Example:***
    - *Negative Thought: "I always mess things up."*
    - *Reframe: "I make mistakes, but I also learn and grow from them."*

5. Limiting Beliefs Challenge:
  - ***Exercise:*** Identify any limiting beliefs you hold about yourself. Write them down, then challenge each belief with evidence to the contrary.
  - ***Example:***
    - *Limiting Belief: "I'm not good enough."*
    - *Challenge: List accomplishments, positive feedback, or instances where you felt proud of yourself.*

6. Daily Gratitude Practice:
  - ***Exercise:*** Sow seeds of gratitude in your life by jotting down three things you're grateful for each day. This practice shifts your focus toward the positive aspects of your life and is key in helping you learn how to see the blessing in every lesson.
  - ***Reflection:***
    - *How does expressing gratitude impact my mood and perspective?*
    - *In what ways can I appreciate myself as part of this daily practice?*

7. Visualization Exercise:
- ***Exercise:*** Close your eyes and visualize a version of yourself who exudes confidence and self-assurance. Picture the way you stand, speak, and interact with others. What are you wearing? Where are you standing? Make the details as specific and vivid as possible. Use this mental image as inspiration.
  - ***Reflection:***
    - *How does this visualization make me feel about myself?*
    - *What small steps can I take to embody this confident version of myself?*

8. Compliment Jar:
- ***Exercise:*** Create a compliment jar where you write down compliments or positive feedback you receive. When feeling low, revisit the compliments to boost your self-esteem. Do not throw away the compliments once you've read them. They are forever yours to keep and to remind yourself of the way your beauty shows up in the world. These compliments are the various ways your light shines in the life of others.
  - ***Questions for Reflection:***
    - *How do these compliments reflect my strengths and positive qualities?*
    - *In what ways can I internalize and believe these positive affirmations?*

Building a positive self-image is an ongoing process, and with time and dedication, you can create a more resilient and confident sense of self. Please approach these exercises with patience and consistency. They are designed to help you heal those inner wounds. You are teaching yourself how to see every part of you. Not just the part you feel. It will take time to change how you think of yourself and what you truly see when you look at yourself. Not the physical attributes but who you SEE when you look in the mirror or catch a glimpse of a reflection when you are out and about. Love takes time.

Practicing self-compassion and forgiveness:
Self-compassion and forgiveness are crucial components of the journey toward emotional healing. It is important to be understanding and kind to yourself in moments of difficulty or perceived failure. You will be guided through forgiveness exercises, helping you release emotional baggage tied

to past experiences and mistakes. You will explore the correlation between self-compassion, forgiveness, and overall emotional well-being, encouraging you to treat yourself with the same kindness and forgiveness you extend to others.

Forgiveness Exercises for Releasing Emotional Baggage:
1. Letter Writing: Self-Forgiveness Edition:
- *Exercise:* Write a compassionate letter to yourself, acknowledging mistakes and expressing forgiveness. Outline the lessons learned and commit to moving forward with self-love.
  - *Tips:*
    - Be honest about your feelings and actions.
    - Remind yourself of the factors that led to that event.
    - Include what could have been done differently on your part, if anything.
    - Focus on understanding rather than self-judgment.

2. Timeline of Forgiveness:
- *Exercise:* Create a timeline of significant events in your life, noting where forgiveness is needed. Reflect on each event, and consider forgiving yourself for any perceived shortcomings. If you are having difficulty forgiving yourself, do not be afraid to dig deeper into that. You may be holding onto emotions from situations that are creating the framework for how you perceive yourself.
  - *Reflection:*
    - How has the lack of forgiveness impacted my emotional well-being?
    - What does forgiveness in each instance look like for me?
- *Exercise:* Practice a self-compassion meditation. In a quiet space, focus on your breath, acknowledging any negative feelings. Gradually, replace self-critical thoughts with words of understanding and forgiveness. Replace those thoughts with words of love and understanding for your self.
  - *Affirmations:*
    - "I am human, and I make mistakes. It's okay."
    - "I forgive myself for the past and embrace my journey of growth."

4. Symbolic Release Ritual:
- *Exercise:* Choose a symbolic item representing your emotional baggage. Write down what you want to release, attach it to the item, and find a meaningful way to release or dispose of it.

- *Reflection:*
  - How does this symbolic release impact my sense of emotional liberation?
  - What emotions arise during this ritual?

5. Reflection on Compassionate Moments:
- *Exercise:* Reflect on moments in your life where you demonstrated self-compassion. How did you treat yourself with kindness during challenging times? Use these reflections to guide forgiveness for past mistakes.
- *Questions:*
  - How can I extend the same compassion to myself in moments of difficulty?
  - What self-soothing techniques have worked for me in the past?

6. The Power of Affirmations:
- *Exercise:* Develop forgiveness-focused affirmations. Repeat these affirmations daily to reinforce a mindset of self-forgiveness and acceptance.
- *Affirmations:*
  - "I am worthy of giving myself forgiveness and love."
  - "I release the past and embrace the present with compassion."

7. Gratitude for Lessons Learned:
- *Exercise:* List the valuable lessons you've learned from past mistakes. Express gratitude for the growth and wisdom gained from these experiences.
  - *Reflection:*
    - *How have these lessons shaped my current self?*
    - *In what ways can I appreciate the transformative power of mistakes?*

8. Empathy Journaling:
- *Exercise:* Write about the situation for which you seek forgiveness as if you were a close friend. Offer empathy, understanding, and forgiveness from an outsider's perspective. What would you say to your friend? How would you want your friend to process the situation?
  - *Tips:*
    - *Use a compassionate and understanding tone.*
    - *Focus on the growth and resilience displayed.*

9. Release Through Art:
- *Exercise:* Engage in a creative outlet such as drawing, painting, or sculpting to express the emotions tied to your forgiveness journey. Allow the process to be cathartic and freeing.
  - *Reflection:*
    - *How does the act of creation contribute to my emotional release?*
    - *What emotions are conveyed through the artwork?*

10. Guided Forgiveness Meditation:
- *Exercise:* Follow a guided meditation specifically designed for forgiveness. Focus on self-forgiveness, letting go of resentment, and embracing a compassionate perspective.
  - *Reflection:*
    - *How does this meditation impact my sense of inner peace?*
    - *What emotions arise during the process?*

Remember: Forgiveness is a process. Not an immediate destination. Remind yourself that self-compassion is a vital aspect of overall emotional well-being. Using a variety of these techniques will allow you to forgive and heal various aspects of your inner self as well as your heart. You have to learn how to forgive yourself so you can truly trust and believe in yourself. Forgiving yourself is a part of uncovering your truth. There is no need to hide in the shadows because of errors from your past. You are an incredible human being with a heart worthy and deserving of real love.

Strategies for boosting self-esteem and nurturing self-love:

Practical strategies for boosting self-esteem and nurturing self-love are the focus of this section. You will begin to develop a personalized self-care routine that aligns with your preferences and needs. Additionally, you will be provided with strategies for further establishing a growth mindset and shifting your perspective to see setbacks as opportunities for learning and growth. In order for you to be successful, you will have to actively participate in your own self-esteem building journey, nurturing a deeper sense of self-love and appreciation.

Practical Strategies for Boosting Self-Esteem and Nurturing Self-Love:
1. Set and Achieve Small Goals:
- *Strategy:* Break down larger goals into smaller, manageable tasks. Celebrate each achievement, reinforcing a sense of competence and capability.
  - *Action Steps:*
    - *Identify a small goal for the week.*
    - *Break it down into achievable steps.*
    - *Acknowledge and celebrate each step.*

2. Engage in Daily Affirmations:
- *Strategy:* Incorporate positive affirmations into your daily routine. Use statements that promote self-love, resilience, and confidence.
  - *Action Steps:*
    - *Create a list of affirmations.*
    - *Repeat them in the morning or before bedtime.*
    - *Believe in and internalize the affirmations.*

3. Develop a Personalized Self-Care Routine:
  - *Strategy:* Tailor a self-care routine to your preferences and needs. Include activities that bring joy, relaxation, and fulfillment.
  - *Action Steps:*
    - *Identify self-care activities you enjoy.*
    - *Schedule dedicated time for self-care.*
    - *Experiment with different practices to find what resonates.*

4. Seek Positive Affirmations from Supportive Sources:
  - *Strategy:* Surround yourself with positive and supportive individuals who provide genuine affirmations. Seek constructive feedback that reinforces your strengths.
  - *Action Steps:*
    - *Share your goals with supportive friends or family.*
    - *Ask for affirmations and encouragement.*
    - *Express gratitude for their support.*

5. Cultivate a Growth Mindset:
  - *Strategy:* Embrace challenges and view setbacks as opportunities for learning and growth. Adopt a mindset that values effort and persistence.
  - *Action Steps:*
    - *Reflect on challenges as learning experiences.*
    - *Focus on the process rather than just outcomes.*
    - *Celebrate efforts and improvements.*

6. Journaling for Self-Reflection:
  - *Strategy:* Maintain a journal to reflect on your thoughts, feelings, and achievements. Use it as a tool for self-discovery and self-expression.
  - *Action Steps:*
    - *Set aside time for regular journaling.*
    - *Write about positive experiences and accomplishments.*
    - *Explore areas for personal growth.*

7. Practice Self-Compassion:
  - *Strategy:* Treat yourself with the same kindness and understanding that you would offer to a friend. Be gentle in moments of difficulty.

- *Action Steps:*
  - *Notice self-critical thoughts and challenge them.*
  - *Offer words of comfort to yourself in challenging times.*
  - *Acknowledge that mistakes are part of the human experience.*

8. Affirm Your Strengths and Achievements:
- *Strategy:* Create a list of your strengths, achievements, and positive qualities. Refer to this list when self-doubt arises.
- *Action Steps:*
  - *Regularly update your list of strengths.*
  - *Remind yourself of past achievements.*
  - *Focus on your abilities and qualities*

9. Connect with a Supportive Community:
- *Strategy:* Engage with communities or groups that share your interests and values. Building connections with like-minded individuals can boost self-esteem.
- *Action Steps:*
  - *Join clubs, groups, or online communities.*
  - *Participate in discussions and share experiences.*
  - *Offer support to others and receive it in return.*

10. Celebrate Your Unique Qualities:
- *Strategy:* Embrace and celebrate your uniqueness. Recognize that your individuality is a source of strength and beauty.
- *Action Steps:*
  - *Make a list of qualities that make you unique.*
  - *Celebrate your quirks and differences.*
  - *Share your unique perspective with others.*

By actively participating in your self-esteem building journey, you will gain the tools needed to obtain a deeper sense of self-love, appreciation, and overall well-being. Your love for yourself is growing. Your confidence in yourself is growing. You are learning to see yourself in a brighter light. You are learning to forgive yourself. You are learning to speak to the portions of you that have been hidden. You are finding your voice.

Chapter 6:

Healthy Relationship Mindset

Healthy Relationship Mindset

Understanding the importance of a healthy mindset in attracting positive relationships:
   Recognizing the profound impact that a healthy mindset can have on attracting positive and fulfilling relationships, you will be guided to understand the connection between your thoughts, beliefs, and the quality of relationships you attract. You will be encouraged to develop a positive and optimistic outlook through the law of attraction. Through a series of practical exercises designed to help you shift your mindset toward openness, abundance, and the belief in the possibility of positive connections, you will begin to develop the skills to see situations in a different light. A healthier, more positive light. Building on the work you've done from previous exercises, continue to push into some of the unchartered portions of your past.

Cultivating a Healthy Relationship Mindset:
1. Understanding the Mind-Relationship Connection:
   - *Concept:* Recognize the link between your thoughts, beliefs, and the quality of relationships you attract. Understand that your mindset shapes your perception and experiences in relationships. Again, this is not a time to beat yourself up for previous relationships or the quality of those relationships. This is to help you recognize any patterns you may have so that you can become aware of your own behaviors.
   - *Exploration:*
      - Reflect on past relationships and identify recurring thought patterns.
      - Consider how your beliefs about love and relationships have influenced your experiences.

2. Law of Attraction in Relationships:
   - *Concept:* Explore the concept of the law of attraction in the context of relationships. Acknowledge that your energy and beliefs can attract similar energies and beliefs in others.
   - *Action Steps:*
      - Research and understand the principles of the law of attraction.
      - Reflect on instances where your mindset may have influenced relationship dynamics.

3. Shifting Negative Thought Patterns:

- *Exercise:* Identify and challenge negative thought patterns related to relationships. Replace them with positive and empowering thoughts that align with the kind of relationship you desire.
   - *Example:*
     - Negative Thought: "I always attract the wrong kind of people."
     - Positive Reframe: "I am learning from past experiences and attracting positive connections."

4. **Visualizing Positive Relationship Outcomes:**
   - *Exercise:* Engage in visualization exercises to imagine positive and fulfilling relationship scenarios. Picture yourself in a healthy, loving, and supportive partnership. It does not matter if it is a fairytale or something you've never witnessed personally. It could also be scenarios from previous relationships. The point is to imagine yourself in positive, healthy scenarios. Allow your mind to become the vision board for that future healthy relationship. This is your time to be selfish and demanding with your choices. You know what you deserve and are worthy of having in your life
   - *Steps:*
     - Find a quiet space for visualization.
     - Envision specific details of a positive relationship.
     - Allow positive emotions associated with this vision to permeate your thoughts.

5. **Relationship Affirmations:**
   - *Exercise:* Craft positive affirmations specifically focused on relationships. Repeat these affirmations regularly to reinforce a positive and open mindset.
   - *Affirmations:*
     - "I am deserving of a loving and fulfilling relationship."
     - "Positive connections come into my life effortlessly."
     - "I attract relationships that align with my values and bring joy."

6. Cultivating Gratitude for Relationships:
  - *Exercise:* Develop a gratitude practice centered around relationships. Express gratitude for positive connections, even if they are not romantic. This practice helps you appreciate the relationships you have as well as the types of relationships you have.
  - *Reflection:*
    - Journal about the positive relationships in your life.
    - Focus on the qualities you appreciate in these connections.

7. Journaling for Relationship Clarity:
  - *Exercise:* Journal about your ideal relationship. Be specific about your values, desires, and the emotional experience you seek in a partnership. This exercise helps refine and define your mindset and intentions.
  - *Prompts:*
    - Describe the qualities of your ideal partner.
    - Explore the emotions you want to experience in a relationship.

8. Affirming Self-Love as a Magnet for Positive Relationships:
  - *Concept:* Recognize that curating self-love acts as a magnet for positive relationships. Embrace self-love as the foundation for attracting connections that align with your well-being. Do not rush through this process. Again, this may feel a little uncomfortable but take this time to love you. All of you. You know you better than anyone else. It is time to reacquaint yourself with all of the beauty that lies within you.
  - *Action Steps:*
    - Identify practices that promote self-love.
    - Recognize how self-love positively impacts your interactions with others.

9. Integrating Abundance Mindset:
  - *Concept:* Embrace an abundance mindset in relationships. Trust that there are ample opportunities for positive connections and the right relationship will come into your life at the right time. With all of the amazing you may have experienced before, do not believe that was a once in a lifetime feeling or occurrence. It may not occur with the person you initially envisioned but it does not mean it will never or can never happen again. Abundance. Your cup will runneth over…and so will your future partner's.
  - *Reflection:*
    - Challenge scarcity beliefs about relationships.

- Focus on the abundance of positive qualities within yourself and potential partners.

10. Practicing Mindful Presence in Relationships:
  - *Concept:* Understand the importance of mindful presence when creating positive connections. Be fully engaged and present in your interactions, allowing for authentic and meaningful connections.
  - *Action Steps:*
    - Practice mindfulness in daily activities.
    - Be present and attentive in conversations and social interactions.

Consistent practice of these exercises will shift your mindset toward openness, abundance, and the belief in the possibility of positive connections. As your healthy relationship mindset grows, you enhance your ability to attract and nurture fulfilling relationships in your life. Not just romantically but through all aspects of your life. In doing this entire process, you are creating new boundaries, expectations, and aspirations for yourself. There may be people around you that do not understand the changes you are making for yourself. That is okay. But also know that if people around you can notice the changes, you are definitely growing within yourself and shining brighter for those around you to see.

Letting go of unrealistic expectations and embracing vulnerability:
   To create healthier relationships, it is essential to address your unrealistic expectations and embrace vulnerability. This section will lead you through the process of identifying and reevaluating expectations that may be setting you up for disappointment. Practical exercises, such as creating a realistic list of relationship expectations and exploring the concept of imperfection are provided amongst additional exercises. It is important to be able to embrace vulnerability as a strength, allowing for genuine connection and intimacy. By letting go of rigid expectations and opening oneself to vulnerability, you will be able to create a more authentic and sustainable foundation for positive relationships.

Embracing Realistic Expectations and Vulnerability in Relationships:
1. Identifying Unrealistic Expectations:
  - *Exercise:* Reflect on past relationships and identify patterns of disappointment. Examine expectations that may have contributed to these disappointments.
  - *Steps:*
    - Journal about instances of disappointment in past relationships.
    - Identify the expectations that were unmet.

- Question whether these expectations were realistic.
  -Determine how, when, and where those expectations were created.

2. Creating a Realistic Expectations List:
  - *Exercise:* Develop a list of realistic expectations for relationships. Differentiate between essential qualities and preferences, focusing on realistic and achievable aspects.
    - *Guidelines:*
      - Prioritize qualities that contribute to a healthy relationship.
      - Distinguish between negotiable and non-negotiable expectations.

3. Exploring the Concept of Imperfection:
  - *Exercise:* Challenge the pursuit of perfection in relationships by exploring the concept of imperfection. Acknowledge that imperfections are a natural part of being human. Imperfections are what make you unique.
    - *Reflection:*
      - Consider how society's ideals of perfection influence expectations.
      - Reflect on how imperfections contribute to depth and authenticity.

4. Journaling About Vulnerability:
  - *Exercise:* Journal about your thoughts and feelings regarding vulnerability. Explore the fears and benefits associated with being vulnerable in relationships.
    - *Prompts:*
      - How do I define vulnerability?
      - What fears or hesitations do I have about being vulnerable?
      - How can vulnerability contribute to authentic connections?
      - How do I feel about my partner being vulnerable with me?

5. Shifting from Perfection to Authenticity:
  - *Concept:* Understand that perfection is an unrealistic standard. Shift the focus from perfection to authenticity as the foundation for genuine connections.
    - *Action Steps:*
      - Recognize the beauty in your imperfections.
      - Embrace authenticity as a source of strength in relationships.

6. Practicing Vulnerability Exercises:
  - *Exercise:* Engage in vulnerability exercises to gradually open up. Share personal experiences, thoughts, or feelings with someone you trust. Work on building a deeper connection with someone you already trust.

- *Examples:*
    - Share a personal story of overcoming a challenge.
    - Express your feelings about a topic that matters to you.

7. Communication Skills for Expressing Vulnerability:
- *Concept:* Develop effective communication skills to express vulnerability. Learn to communicate feelings and needs in a way that encourages understanding and connection.
    - *Skills to Develop:*
        - Use "I" statements to express emotions.
        - Practice active listening to enhance understanding.

8. Setting Boundaries While Being Vulnerable:
- *Concept:* Understand that vulnerability doesn't mean relinquishing boundaries. Establish and communicate clear boundaries while still being open and authentic in your interactions.
    - *Guidelines:*
        - Reflect on your personal boundaries.
        - Communicate boundaries with respect and clarity.

9. Embracing Imperfections in Others:
- *Exercise:* Challenge judgments and expectations placed on others. Embrace the imperfections of potential partners, recognizing that everyone has strengths and areas for growth.
    - *Reflection:*
        - Consider how accepting imperfections contributes to healthier relationships.
        - Reflect on the qualities that truly matter in a partner.

10. Mindfulness Practices for Embracing the Present Moment:
- *Exercise:* Engage in mindfulness practices to stay present in relationships. Let go of future expectations and embrace the beauty of the present moment.
    - *Practices:*
        - Mindful breathing during conversations.
        - Grounding exercises to stay present.

Self-reflection and growth are a continuous process in the evolution of expectations and vulnerability in relationships. By embracing realistic expectations and vulnerability, you pave the way for authentic connections and encourage healthier, more sustainable relationships in your life.

Developing resilience in the face of challenges in romantic relationships:

Challenges are inevitable in any relationship, and developing resilience is crucial for navigating these inevitable ups and downs. This section examines the concept of relationship resilience and provides a variety of strategies for building emotional strength. You will learn how to manage conflicts constructively, effective communication strategies, and view challenges as opportunities for growth rather than threats to the relationship. There is also a brief exploration into the importance of self-care during challenging times and the role of mutual support in developing resilience.

Building Relationship Resilience: Navigating Challenges with Emotional Strength

1. Understanding Relationship Resilience:
   - *Concept:* Define relationship resilience as the capacity to withstand and recover from challenges, fostering growth and strength.

   - *Exploration:*
      - Reflect on past relationship challenges and how they were navigated.
      - Recognize the role of resilience in overcoming difficulties.

2. Communication Strategies for Emotional Strength:
   - *Concept:* Effective communication is a cornerstone of resilience. Learn to express yourself and listen actively, creating the space for understanding and connection.
   - *Strategies:*
      - Use "I" statements to express feelings.
      - Practice reflective listening to ensure understanding.
      - Foster an open and non-judgmental communication environment.

3. Conflict Management for Constructive Resolution:
   -*Concept:* Conflict is natural; how you manage it determines resilience. Approach conflicts as opportunities for growth and resolution.
   - *Guidelines:*
      - Focus on the issue, not personal attacks.
      - Determine how to collaborate on finding solutions.
      - Prioritize compromise over winning.

4. Viewing Challenges as Growth Opportunities:
   - *Concept:* Reframe challenges as opportunities for personal and relational growth. Adopt a mindset that embraces learning and development.
   - *Actions:*
     - Journal about challenges as opportunities.
     - Journal about the lessons learned from past difficulties with previous partners.

5. Self-Care During Challenging Times:
   - *Concept:* Prioritize self-care to maintain emotional well-being during relationship challenges. Think beyond the mundane. Include guilty pleasures as rewards for accomplishing or working through certain situations (mentally, emotionally, or physically).
   - *Practices:*
     - Establish a self-care routine.
     - Identify activities that bring comfort and relaxation.
     - How would you communicate your self-care needs to your partner?

6. Cultivating Mutual Support:
   - *Concept:* Mutual support is a pillar of relationship resilience. Building an environment where both partners actively support each other and feel safe are fundamental for the overall health of the relationship.
   - *Strategies:*
     - Share vulnerabilities and ask for support.
     - Acknowledge and appreciate each other's efforts.
     - Collaborate on problem-solving.

7. Developing Emotional Regulation Skills:
   - *Concept:* Strengthen emotional regulation to navigate challenges calmly and constructively. Ideally, it is not the goal to put your partner in defensive mode. Nothing can be heard or settled when either of you feel attacked. Becoming more aware of your own emotions will help you to better navigate your own actions and reactions.
   - *Skills to Develop:*
     - Practice mindfulness for emotional awareness.
     - Learn techniques for calming oneself during stress.
     - Explore relaxation methods like deep breathing.

8. Creating Shared Goals for Resilience:

- *Concept:* Establish shared goals that focus on building resilience as a couple.
  - *Actions:*
    - Discuss and set relationship goals during calm periods.
    - Create a plan for navigating challenges together.

9. Learning from Past Resilience:
- *Exercise:* Reflect on past instances of resilience in your relationship. Identify strengths and coping mechanisms that can be applied in future challenges.
  - *Questions to Consider:*
    - How did we navigate past challenges successfully?
    - What strengths did we exhibit during those times?

10. Seeking Professional Support When Needed:
- *Concept:* Recognize the value of professional support during particularly challenging times.
  - *Actions:*
    - Consider couples counseling for additional guidance.
    - Normalize seeking external support as a proactive step.

Although you may not be in a couple at the moment, having these strategies in your arsenal will only help strengthen various facets of your relationship in the future. By beginning to encourage a proactive and collaborative approach to building resilience in your relationship, these strategies may become more of a habit or reflex over time. By implementing these various strategies in your relationships, you can learn to navigate challenges with emotional strength, promote growth, and deepen the bond with your future partner.

Chapter 7:

Tools for Emotional Healing

Tools for Emotional Healing

Therapeutic approaches for emotional healing:
   This section introduces various therapeutic approaches that can aid in emotional healing. It opens the discussion to different modalities such as cognitive-behavioral therapy (CBT), dialectical behavior therapy (DBT), and psychodynamic therapy as tools for emotional healing. This section explains how these approaches may help you explore and address the root causes of emotional heartbreak, providing practical tools for reshaping thought patterns and behaviors. There are additional options available. Make sure you find the option that best suits you and your needs. No one knows what you need better than you. Be willing to explore a variety of options. An approach that seems completely foreign to you may end up being exactly what you need. This is your time to listen to you and explore you and understand you. There are no wrong answers. Every attempt results in an answer. That answer allows you to build a greater, deeper bond with and understanding of your inner you.

Exploring Therapeutic Approaches for Emotional Healing:
1. Introduction to Cognitive-Behavioral Therapy (CBT):
   - *Overview:* CBT is a goal-oriented therapeutic approach that explores the connection between thoughts, feelings, and behaviors. It equips individuals with practical tools to identify and reshape negative thought patterns.
   - *Application:* Learn how CBT can be applied to understand and transform thought patterns contributing to emotional heartbreak.

2. Navigating Emotional Challenges with Dialectical Behavior Therapy (DBT):
   - *Overview:* DBT combines cognitive-behavioral techniques with mindfulness strategies. It's particularly effective in managing intense emotions and improving interpersonal effectiveness.
   - *Application:* Explore how DBT can help regulate emotions and enhance interpersonal skills to address emotional heartbreak.

3. Unveiling the Depths with Psychodynamic Therapy:
   - *Overview:* Psychodynamic therapy delves into unconscious processes and unresolved conflicts. It offers insights into the root causes of emotional challenges and aims for long-term change.
   - *Application:* Understand how psychodynamic therapy can uncover and address underlying issues contributing to emotional heartbreak.

4. Reshaping Thought Patterns with Rational Emotive Behavior Therapy (REBT):
   - *Overview:* REBT focuses on identifying and challenging irrational beliefs that contribute to emotional distress. It emphasizes cognitive restructuring to promote emotional well-being.
   - *Application:* Learn how REBT techniques can help reshape thought patterns and foster emotional resilience.

5. Mindfulness-Based Cognitive Therapy (MBCT):
   - *Overview:* MBCT integrates mindfulness practices into cognitive therapy. It aims to prevent the recurrence of depressive episodes by cultivating mindfulness and awareness.
   - *Application:* Explore how MBCT can enhance self-awareness and break the cycle of negative thinking associated with emotional heartbreak.

6. Narrative Therapy for Rewriting Your Story:
   - *Overview:* Narrative therapy views individuals as storytellers of their lives. It helps reframe personal narratives, empowering individuals to redefine their experiences.
   - *Application:* Understand how narrative therapy can assist in reconstructing a narrative that promotes healing and resilience.

7. Holistic Healing with Gestalt Therapy:
   - *Overview:* Gestalt therapy focuses on the present moment and emphasizes personal responsibility. It uses experiential techniques to integrate fragmented aspects of the self.
   - *Application:* Discover how gestalt therapy can provide a holistic approach to addressing emotional heartbreak by promoting self-awareness and integration.

8. Acceptance and Commitment Therapy (ACT):
- *Overview:* ACT combines acceptance and mindfulness strategies with commitment to behavior change. It encourages individuals to accept what is beyond their control and commit to actions aligned with their values.
- *Application:* Explore how ACT can help individuals move beyond emotional pain and commit to a life in line with their values.

9. Solution-Focused Brief Therapy (SFBT):
- *Overview:* SFBT is future-focused, emphasizing solutions rather than problems. It helps individuals identify and build on their strengths to create positive change.
- *Application:* Learn how SFBT can provide practical solutions and create a positive trajectory for overcoming emotional challenges.

10. Holistic Wellness with Integrative Therapy:
- *Overview:* Integrative therapy incorporates multiple therapeutic approaches tailored to individual needs. It recognizes the interconnectedness of emotional, physical, and spiritual well-being.
- *Application:* Understand the benefits of integrative therapy in fostering holistic wellness and addressing emotional heartbreak from various angles.

Please be advised this is a sample of different therapeutic modalities that you can further explore, if you choose. These various therapeutic approaches can provide valuable insight and additional practical tools to aid you on your journey of emotional healing.

Mindfulness and meditation practices:
Mindfulness and meditation are powerful tools for cultivating emotional well-being. Techniques such as guided meditation, mindful breathing, and body scan exercises are explored to help you become more present and attuned to your emotions. Incorporating these principles of mindfulness and meditation can enhance self-awareness, reduce stress, and contribute to a more balanced emotional state. Simple mindfulness exercises and tips for integrating mindfulness into daily routines are provided, making these practices accessible for you at various levels of experience.

Embracing Mindfulness: A Path to Self-Awareness and Emotional Balance

Principles of Mindfulness:
1. Present Moment Awareness:

- *Principle:* Mindfulness involves being fully present in the current moment, acknowledging thoughts and feelings without judgment.
- *Application:* Practice focusing on your immediate experience rather than dwelling on the past or anticipating the future.

2. Non-Judgmental Observation:
- *Principle:* Mindfulness encourages observing thoughts and emotions without attaching labels of good or bad.
- *Application:* Cultivate an attitude of curiosity and acceptance towards your thoughts and feelings during mindful practices.

3. Mindful Breathing:
- *Principle:* Breath serves as an anchor to the present moment. Mindful breathing involves paying attention to the breath with intention.
- *Application:* Incorporate conscious breathing exercises to center yourself and cultivate awareness.

4. Acceptance of Impermanence:
- *Principle:* Mindfulness recognizes the transient nature of thoughts and emotions. It encourages acceptance of change.
- *Application:* Reflect on the impermanence of emotions during mindfulness, fostering a sense of detachment from momentary challenges.

Practical Guidance on Meditation Practices:
1. Guided Meditation:
- *Technique:* Utilize recorded or live guided meditations led by experienced instructors. They provide verbal cues and imagery to guide your meditation.
- *Application:* Find guided meditations focused on topics such as self-compassion, gratitude, or emotional healing.

2. Mindful Breathing Exercises:
- *Technique:* Engage in intentional breathing patterns, such as diaphragmatic breathing or box breathing, to bring attention to the breath.
- *Application:* Dedicate a few minutes daily to mindful breathing, gradually extending the duration as you become more comfortable.

3. Body Scan Meditation:
- *Technique:* Systematically scan your body, paying attention to sensations, tension, and relaxation from head to toe.
- *Application:* Practice a body scan as part of your bedtime routine to promote relaxation and release physical tension.

Benefits of Mindfulness in Daily Life:
1. Enhanced Self-Awareness:
- *Tip: Set aside a few moments each day to check in with yourself, observing your thoughts and emotions without judgment.*

2. Stress Reduction:
- *Tip: During moments of stress, pause and focus on your breath for a few minutes to ground yourself and create a sense of calm.*

3. Emotional Regulation:
- *Tip: When facing intense emotions, practice mindful breathing to create space and respond more intentionally rather than reactively.*

Integrating Mindfulness into Daily Routines:
1. Mindful Moments:
- *Tip: Infuse mindfulness into routine activities, such as mindful walking, eating, or even washing dishes by paying full attention to each action.*

2. Mindfulness Apps:
- *Tip: Explore mindfulness apps that offer guided meditations, mindful exercises, and reminders to help you incorporate mindfulness into your day.*

3. Mindful Reflection:
- *Tip: Before bed, engage in a short mindful reflection on the day, acknowledging both challenges and moments of gratitude.*

Embracing mindfulness is a transformative journey towards self-awareness and emotional balance. Integrating mindfulness into your daily life will allow for a more mindful and centered approach to your emotions. Whether you are new to mindfulness or have some experience, these principles and practices can be tailored to meet you where you are on your journey.

Seeking support from friends, family, or professional counselors:
The importance of seeking support is a fundamental tool for emotional healing. Although it may be difficult at times, you are encouraged to lean on your social support networks, including friends and family, for emotional assistance. Through the tools previously taught, you will be able to effectively communicate with loved ones, express your needs, and build a reliable support system. However, friends and family should not be the only ones in your support system. Seeking professional counseling will help to address any concerns or mental obstacles that are not addressed in this guide. Healing is a personal journey; however, it is not a solo journey. There are trained professionals and loved ones who are willing to assist. Create the community and support system you need to withstand the journey you are on.

Chapter 8:

Realizing Your Wonderful Self

Realizing Your Wonderful Self

Embracing the journey of personal growth and transformation:
   The journey toward realizing your wonderful self is an ongoing process of personal growth and transformation. Life is a continuous exploration of learning, adapting, and evolving. It is important to understand the concept of a growth mindset while recognizing that challenges and setbacks are opportunities for learning and self-discovery. Techniques for setting realistic personal goals, cultivating new skills, and embracing change are provided to empower you on this lifelong journey. Many of these strategies will be familiar to you but will be applied in a different manner. Remain open minded now and throughout your days to come. The beauty of this journey will unfold in ways that are currently unimaginable.

Embracing a Growth Mindset: A Pathway to Learning and Self-Discovery

Understanding the Growth Mindset:
 1. Mindset Foundations:
   - *Concept:* A growth mindset embraces the belief that abilities can be developed through dedication and hard work. Challenges are viewed as opportunities for growth, not as indicators of failure.

 2. Embracing Challenges:
   - *Principle:* Challenges are seen as stepping stones to learning and improvement, fostering resilience and a positive attitude towards overcoming obstacles.

Practical Tips for Cultivating a Growth Mindset:
 1. Setting Realistic Personal Goals:
   - *Tip:* Break larger goals into smaller, achievable steps. Celebrate small victories, reinforcing the idea that progress is an ongoing journey.

 2. Cultivating New Skills:
   - *Tip:* Approach learning as a continuous process. Start by identifying areas of interest or skills you'd like to develop and dedicate consistent time to practice.

3. Embracing Change:
   - *Tip:* View change as an opportunity for growth rather than a threat. Embrace new experiences and challenges with an open mind, recognizing the potential for learning.

Empowering Self-Discovery Through Growth:
1. Learning from Setbacks:
   - *Approach:* Instead of viewing setbacks as failures, see them as valuable lessons. Reflect on what went wrong, what you've learned, and how you can apply this knowledge moving forward. You can never control how another person responds but you can always control how YOU move forward.

2. Developing Resilience:
   - *Approach:* Build resilience by reframing adversity. Recognize that setbacks do not define you but provide an opportunity to showcase your ability to bounce back stronger. This is your opportunity to learn more about yourself to discover the keys to your future roadblocks.

Tips for Active Participation in Your Growth Journey:
1. Embracing a Learning Mentality:
   - *Encouragement:* Cultivate a curiosity for learning. Ask questions, seek out new information, and approach situations with a willingness to gain knowledge.

2. Seeking Constructive Feedback:
   - *Encouragement:* View feedback as a valuable tool for growth. Seek constructive criticism, and use it to refine your skills and approaches.

3. Fostering a Positive Inner Dialogue:
   - *Encouragement:* Challenge negative self-talk. Replace self-limiting beliefs with affirmations that reinforce your capacity for learning and improvement. Becoming aware of your negative self-talk is growth. Do not overlook that! You are literally learning how to silence the haters that take up space in your mind.

Realizing the Potential for Personal Growth:
1. Reflecting on Progress:
   - *Reflection:* Regularly reflect on your journey. Acknowledge the progress made, identify areas for improvement, and celebrate the continuous effort you invest in your growth. Make this one of your non-negotiables. If you can celebrate others, you can celebrate yourself as well. You deserve the same amount of energy you pour into others to pour into yourself as well.

2. Nurturing a Growth Environment:
   - *Environment:* Surround yourself with supportive individuals who share a growth mindset. Collaborate and learn from others who inspire and encourage personal development. Iron sharpens iron and your journey for personal growth is no different. Your environment can catapult or stifle your efforts. Feed and nourish yourself properly.

3. Embracing the Journey:
   - *Mindset:* Shift your focus from destination-oriented goals to the joy of the journey. Embrace the process of growth, acknowledging that the path itself is a rich and rewarding experience. It is an experience that only YOU will get to fully enjoy.

Through practical tips, reflections, and a positive mindset, you can actively participate in your journey of growth, unlocking your potential and embracing the continuous process of self-improvement. Remember, every challenge and setback are stepping stones on the path to personal development and achievement.

Celebrating progress and small victories:
Recognizing and celebrating progress is crucial for maintaining motivation and sustaining positive change. Acknowledging and celebrating small victories are important milestones in the journey toward emotional healing

and self-discovery. It is important to establish a system for tracking personal achievements, creating a sense of accomplishment, and boosting self-esteem. By learning to appreciate and celebrate incremental progress, you will develop a more positive and resilient attitude toward your journey.

Acknowledging Small Victories: A Key to Emotional Healing and Self-Discovery

Understanding the Significance of Small Victories:
1. Building Blocks of Success:
- *Concept:* Small victories are the foundation of significant achievements. They represent progress and reinforce the idea that positive change is possible. When you acknowledge these victories, you create an inner YES momentum. These victories become reminders that you are successful in your endeavors. They help to build up your self-esteem and renew your confidence in yourself.

2. Boosting Motivation:
- *Principle:* Celebrating small victories provides a motivational boost, encouraging continued effort and dedication to personal growth. Every celebration does not need to be major. What is important is acknowledging that victory both mentally and in some physical manifestation so that you can be reminded of your victory every time you see it. Whatever it is should make you smile every time you see it, hear it, or do it.
Insert happy dance

Establishing a System for Tracking Achievements:
1. Setting Personal Milestones:
- *Tip:* Identify specific, achievable milestones related to emotional healing and self-discovery. Break down larger goals into smaller, manageable steps. This cannot be about healing overnight. It's going to take some time. But taking the necessary steps
now to make those mental changes are what will sustain and form the foundation from which you can further grow.

2. Creating a Progress Journal:
- *Tip:* Maintain a journal to record daily achievements and reflections. Documenting progress provides a tangible record of growth over time. This is really key in being able to see where you were emotionally at the time to where you are at the present. It is difficult to see how you've

grown when there are so many nuances that are not remembered in the day to day of living. A journal captures those moments and emotions that the brain is unable to do with clarity in the future when looking back to the past.

Celebrating Achievements and Cultivating a Sense of Accomplishment:

1. Personalized Rewards:
- *Approach:* Develop a system of rewards for reaching milestones. Choose rewards that resonate with your preferences, creating a positive association with achievement.

2. Expressing Gratitude:
- *Approach:* Voice gratitude for the progress made. Take a moment to acknowledge the effort invested and express gratitude for the support received. If possible, write down in your journal the progress that you've made. Write down how proud of yourself you are for making it as far as you have. It is very important to be your own cheerleader during this time. You have to rebuild trust with yourself before you can truly trust and believe your heart in the future.

Boosting Self-Esteem through Celebration:
1. Positive Self-Talk:
- *Practice:* Replace self-criticism with positive affirmations. Acknowledge your efforts, and intentionally celebrate each step forward. If you had to pay for every negative thought you've had about yourself, how much would you be paying to be mean to you? It may be difficult to think of it in those terms but your money, efforts, and time could be put to better use building yourself up instead of tearing yourself down. You are human. There is nothing in this world that is perfect and that is what makes you beautiful in your own right. No one on this earth can duplicate or replicate YOU. Love on YOU.

2. Sharing Achievements:
- *Approach:* Share your victories with trusted friends or a support network. Celebrating with others enhances the positive impact and fosters a sense of community.

Guidance on Developing a Positive and Resilient Attitude:

1. Learning from Challenges:
- *Mindset:* View challenges as opportunities for growth rather than setbacks. Embrace the lessons learned and recognize the resilience cultivated through overcoming difficulties.

2. Adapting Goals:
- *Mindset:* Be flexible in adjusting goals based on evolving priorities and circumstances. Adaptation is a sign of self-awareness and an essential aspect of the journey.

Encouraging a Culture of Celebration:
1. Encouraging Others:
- *Action:* Celebrate the achievements of those around you. Creating a culture of celebration fosters mutual support and encourages collective growth. Recognizing and acknowledging the achievements of those around you also help you see your own achievements in a different light.

2. Reflecting on Collective Progress:
- *Reflection:* Periodically reflect on your overall progress. Celebrate how far you've come, reinforcing a positive outlook on the journey. Remember to shift those negative experiences and situations towards an honest lesson to be learned. Reflecting on your progress as a whole will help you to recognize your entire journey. Every circumstance, both positive and negative, have built you up to this point. Do not pick it apart. Embrace every portion of your progress.

Guiding you in recognizing and celebrating small victories are crucial milestones in your journey toward emotional healing and self-discovery. By establishing a system for tracking achievements, expressing gratitude, and fostering a positive mindset, you can develop a sense of accomplishment and boost self-esteem. Celebrating progress, no matter how small,
contributes to a resilient attitude, motivating continued effort on the path of personal growth. Remember, each small victory is a testament to your strength and determination.

Shifting the self-perspective from wounded to wonderful:
When you actively participate in your personal growth, you can learn how to shift your self-perspective from one marked by wounds and insecurities to a more positive and wonderful outlook. Practical exercises and

affirmations will help you consciously challenge negative self-talk and replace it with uplifting and positive affirmations. A deeper exploration of self-compassion and utilization of the strategies for developing a kinder self-perspective will enhance your understanding of the relationship you have with yourself. By emphasizing personal strengths, resilience, and the capacity for growth, you will be guided to create a deeper sense of wonder and appreciation for your unique self. Helping you to realize that successfully shifting your self-perspective will inspire and reinforce the idea that transformation is achievable and within reach.

Shifting from Wounded to Wonderful: A Journey of Self-Perspective

1. Challenging Negative Self-Talk:
- *Exercise:* Identify recurring negative thoughts. Challenge each one by asking, "Is this thought based on facts or assumptions?" Replace negative self-talk with positive affirmations. Using this method will also help you recognize your own personal triggers as well as identifying what the feelings and emotions are actually tied to.

2. Affirmations for Empowerment:
- *Practice:* Develop a list of empowering affirmations. Repeat them daily to reinforce a positive self-narrative. Example: "I am resilient. I embrace challenges as opportunities for growth."

3. Embracing Self-Compassion:
- *Strategy:* Encourage self-compassion by treating yourself with the same kindness you would offer a friend facing challenges. Acknowledge mistakes with understanding and a commitment to learn. Become your own best friend.

4. Strategies for Developing Self-Kindness:
- *Technique:* When facing difficulties, ask yourself, "What advice would I give to a friend in this situation?" Apply the same advice to yourself, fostering self-kindness.

5. Emphasizing Personal Strengths:
- *Reflection:* Identify and celebrate your strengths. Reflect on past achievements and instances where you demonstrated resilience. Recognizing personal strengths contributes to a positive self-perspective.

6. Cultivating Resilience:

- ***Practice:*** Develop resilience by reframing challenges as opportunities for growth. Reflect on past difficulties and how you successfully navigated them. Each challenge overcome is a testament to your resilience.

7. Nurturing a Growth Mindset:
- ***Mindset Shift:*** Embrace a growth mindset by viewing setbacks as learning opportunities. Recognize that your abilities can be developed with dedication and effort, fostering a sense of wonder about your potential for growth.

8. Appreciating Unique Qualities:
- ***Exercise:*** Make a list of your unique qualities, talents, and interests. Regularly reflect on this list to appreciate the richness and diversity that makes you wonderfully unique.

9. Daily Gratitude Practice:
- ***Habit Formation:*** Establish a daily gratitude practice. Reflect on three things you are grateful for each day, fostering a positive outlook and appreciation for the wonderful aspects of your life.

10. Celebrating Progress:
- ***Reflection:*** Periodically review your journey. Celebrate the progress made, both big and small. Acknowledge the transformation in your self-perspective as evidence of your capacity for positive change.

Remember, the journey of transformation is within reach and celebrating progress along the way reinforces the idea that positive change is achievable.

Chapter 9:
This Is NOT the End

It is no secret that healing is not easy especially when addressing matters of the heart. There is a lot that goes into reconciling what could have been or what should have been but never was. It is easy to get caught up in feelings of inadequacy but there is something to be said of the power that is gained when you begin to trust and believe in yourself again. The understanding of who you were at the time and the person you've become. As long as you are willing to learn more about yourself to become the person you truly wish to be, not only for yourself but for your future partner, you will learn why those previous relationships did not work. This guide has taken you through a variety of processes including tips that were often repeated. But this is with the understanding that many times steps have to be repeated when you reach a new level of understanding of yourself. Situations and even conversations with yourself can change over time and it's important to address each phase of that healing with the tools you've been provided. This guide has taken you through the importance of self-awareness, the impact of past experiences on emotional well-being, breaking free from people-pleasing, redefining success in relationships, cultivating self-esteem and self-love, adopting a healthy relationship mindset, utilizing tools for emotional healing, and embracing personal growth. The biggest takeaway from all of these steps and tips and new found understandings is that your journey toward emotional healing and self-discovery is not linear. There may be setbacks and overlaps, good days and bad days. However, learning how to give yourself grace and patience while you navigate and explore who you truly are will be the key to building a new today and better tomorrow for who you have decided you are and how you want to show up in the world for yourself and others. As stated below, this guide has walked you through several key components for healing.

1. Increased Self-Awareness: Through various exercises and reflections, you have been given tools that encourage a deeper understanding of yourself, helping you become more aware of your emotions, behaviors, and patterns of thinking.

2. Empowerment in Overcoming Emotional Heartbreak: By exploring therapeutic approaches, mindfulness practices, and seeking support, you have gained practical tools to navigate and overcome emotional heartbreak. Taking back control of your presence, your emotional well-being, is the most liberating, freeing and yet scariest part of this entire transformation. However, the power that lies within you can move mountains, if you allow it.

3. Development of Healthy Relationship Mindset: You have learned to let go of unrealistic expectations, embrace vulnerability, and develop resilience in the face of challenges in romantic relationships. These steps laid the foundation to create a healthy mindset for attracting positive relationships. These steps also taught you how to fall in love with yourself. The most important love there is.

4. Enhanced Self-Esteem and Self-Love: Practical strategies for building a positive self-image, practicing self-compassion, and forgiveness were given. You were empowered to boost your self-esteem and nurture self-love, fostering a more positive relationship with yourself.

5. Redefined Success in Relationships: By evaluating personal definitions of success, shifting focus from external validation to internal fulfillment, and celebrating past successes, you gained a new perspective on what constitutes success in romantic relationships.

6. Tools for Emotional Healing: The introduction of various therapeutic approaches, mindfulness practices, and seeking support as essential tools for emotional healing. You learned how to incorporate these tools into your life for sustained emotional well-being.

7. Realization of a Wonderful Self: Through embracing the journey of personal growth, celebrating progress, and shifting self-perspective from wounded to wonderful, you have embarked on a transformative journey toward realizing your unique and wonderful self.

   Although this guide is comprehensive, it is in no means to be considered encompassing. This is to serve as a source of encouragement for you to continue your journey of self-discovery and personal growth. Your healing journey is a process that is ongoing and each step, no matter how small, contributes to a positive transformation. Never discount or disregard the small steps you have taken. Every step has been intentional and that is what makes you stronger. Those intentional steps help build a solid foundation and framework for who you are becoming or realizing yourself to truly be. You are learning how to go much further than the surface. You are learning how to dig deep and become vulnerable with yourself so you can heal at the root and no longer put a bandage on the outward effects of that pain. Remaining patient and compassionate with yourself as you navigate the complexities of your emotional landscape will give you the space to see how truly beautiful and unique you are. Please remember that self-discovery is a lifelong journey. This guide is a resource to be revisited as often as needed as you progress on your path toward emotional well-being and self-realization.

By inspiring a positive outlook on future romantic relationships, you have learned that the shifts in mindset, the tools for emotional healing, and the practices for self-love are not only applicable to the current moment but are foundational for creating fulfilling and positive connections in the future. These positive connections will spill over into your work, family, and friends as you become more confident and aware of yourself. Your potential for growth in future relationships highlights your journey toward a wonderful self that lays the groundwork for healthier and more satisfying romantic connections.

Taking the journey and necessary steps to go from wounded to wonderful has equipped you with practical strategies and insights to navigate emotional challenges, foster personal growth, and cultivate fulfilling relationships. Although it may not feel like it, you are here because you are strong. You are here because you know you deserve to be loved in the manner in which you choose. You are worthy of all you desire. You had the strength to take the first step towards your healing. So, be reminded: more often than not, the end is just the beginning.

The remainder of this book is empty. This is intentional. This is YOUR blank slate. This is YOUR story. Pour it all out but in a place where you can keep it all together. Your story is greater and longer than the pages that are provided. But remember, this is not the end. This is the beginning. There are no boundaries. No rules. No right or wrong way to express yourself. No right or wrong way to use these pages. Be honest with yourself. Be real. Dispel nightmares. Dare to dream. You are worthy. You are deserving. Do you know why?

Simply because you exist.

I LOVE YOU.

Note to Self:

Note to Self:

Note to Self:

Note to Self:

Note to Self:

Note to Self:

Note to Self:

Note to Self:

Note to Self:

Note to Self:

Note to Self:

Note to Self:

Note to Self:

Note to Self:

Note to Self:

Note to Self:

Note to Self:

Note to Self:

Note to Self:

And a few more things…

Note to Self:

Note to Self:

Note to Self:

…and this too…

Note to Self:

Note to Self:

Note to Self:

…oh…and this too…

Note to Self:

Note to Self:

Note to Self:

Note to Self:

Note to Self:

Note to Self:

Note to Self:

Note to Self:

…and I'm proud of myself for making it here…

Note to Self:

Note to Self:

Note to Self:

Note to Self:

Note to Self:

This may be the last page but far from the final chapter. Keep going.

Made in the USA
Middletown, DE
29 March 2024